Hal Leonard Student Piano Library

Piano Solos

Book 5

Authors
**Barbara Kreader,
Fred Kern, Phillip Keveren**

Consultants
Mona Rejino, Tony Caramia,
Bruce Berr, Richard Rejino

*Director,
Educational Keyboard Publications*
Margaret Otwell

Editor
Carol Klose

Illustrator
Fred Bell

FOREWORD

Piano Solos presents challenging original music that coordinates page-by-page with the **Piano Lessons** books in the **Hal Leonard Student Piano Library**. The outstanding variety of composers and musical styles makes every solo an important piece in its own right – exciting to both performer and listener. In addition, each piece is designed to encourage and ensure further mastery of the concepts and skills in the **Piano Lessons** books.

May these **Piano Solos** become favorite pieces that delight all who hear and play them.

Best wishes,

Barbara Kreader   Fred Kern   Phillip Keveren

ISBN 0-7935-8470-1

HAL•LEONARD®
CORPORATION
7777 W. BLUEMOUND RD. P.O. BOX 13819 MILWAUKEE, WI 53213

Visit Hal Leonard Online at
www.halleonard.com

Piano Solos Book 5

CONTENTS

*✔

Students can check pieces as they play them.

Instrumental Accompaniments for Piano Solos Book 5 are available on:

Compact Disc 🔘   00296071
General MIDI Disk 💾   00296072

The Peppermint Toccata

Fast! ($\bullet$ = 120)

Bruce Berr

3

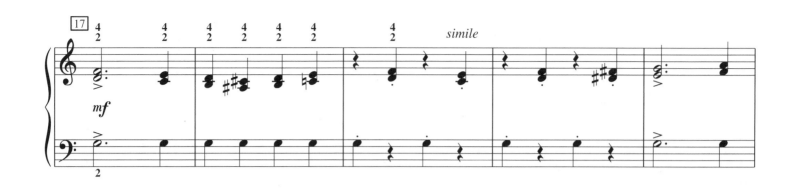

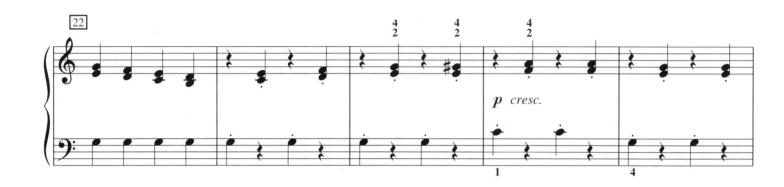

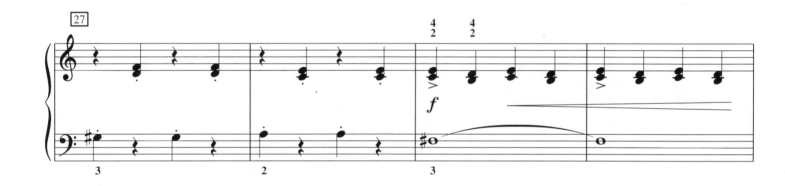

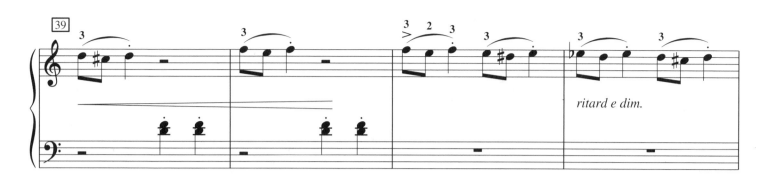

Much slower

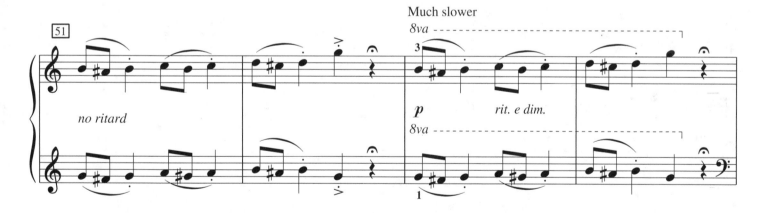

subito - suddenly

5

Snowcrystals

Starlight Song

Calmly (♩ = 50) **5/6** **3**

Bruce Berr

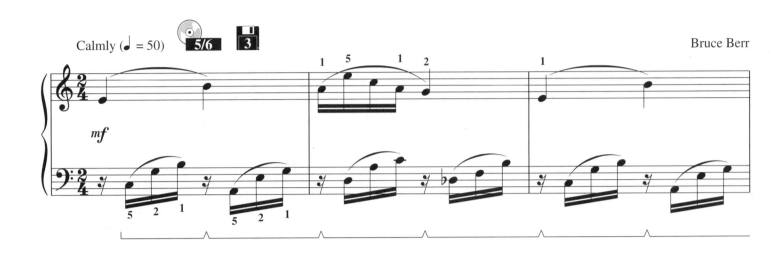

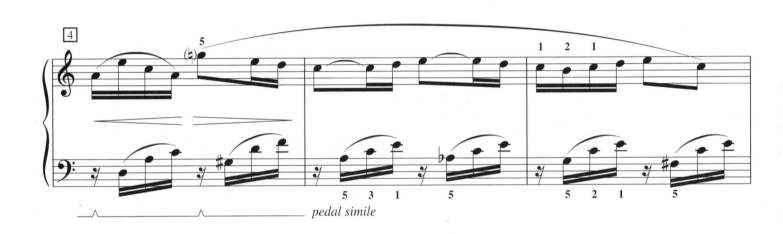

pedal simile

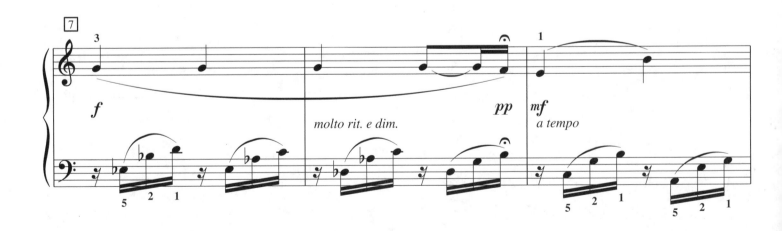

molto rit. e dim.

a tempo

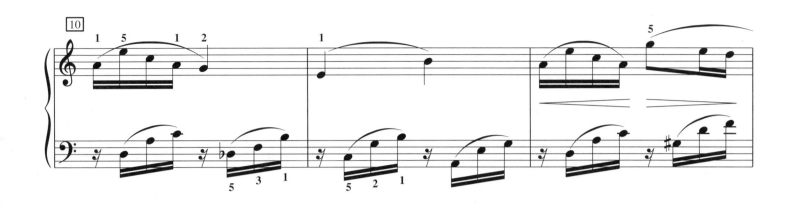

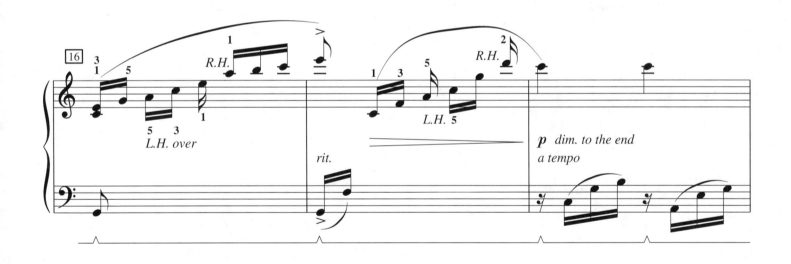

Sailing

On A Grey Day

July

Andante espressivo (♩ = 76) **9/10** **5**

Christos Tsitsaros

The Great Fountain

In "4," fast, with excitement ($\bullet$. = 140)

Bruce Berr

* 𝄻𝄼. - *pedal down*   * - *pedal up*

Use with Lesson Book 5, pg. 18

12

Crystal Clear

Phillip Keveren

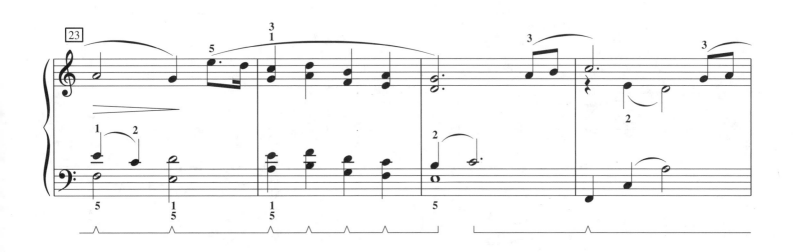

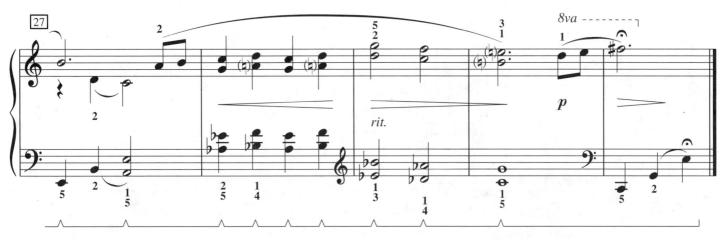

Vaudeville Repartée

With a bounce (♪♫ = ♪ ♪) (♩ = 114) **15/16** **8**

Carol Klose

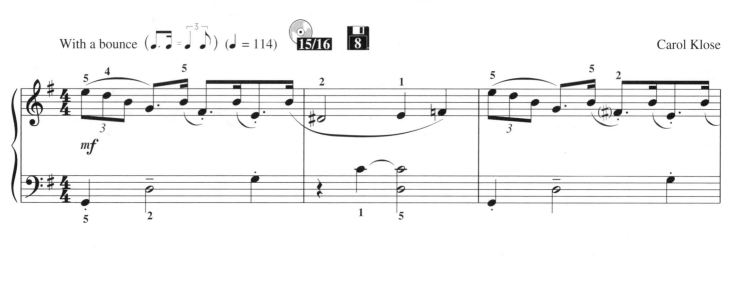

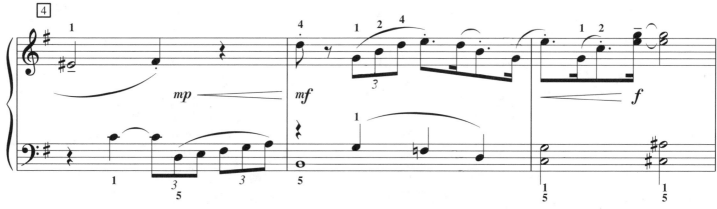

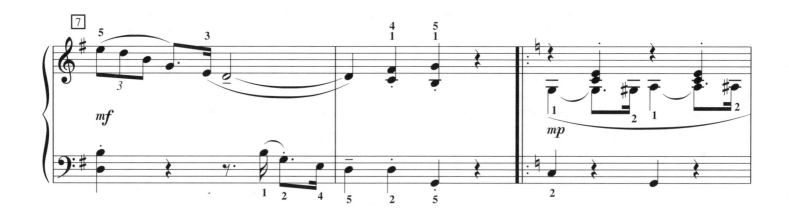

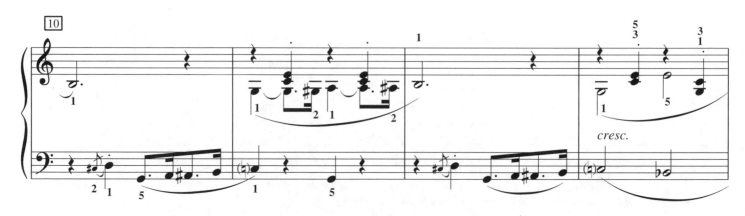

Home Fried Potatoes

Country Rock (♪♪ = ♪♪) (♩ = 126)   **17/18**   **9**

Bill Boyd

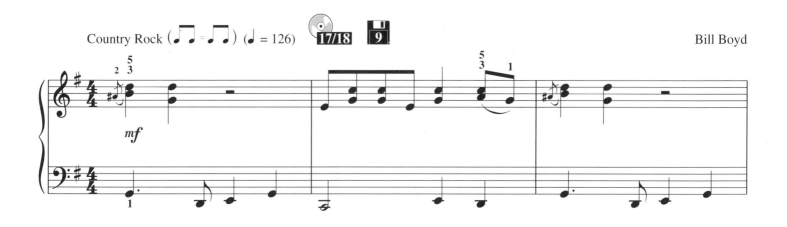

Song Of The Fisherman

Allegro moderato (♩ = 80)   **19/20** **10**   Christos Tsitsaros

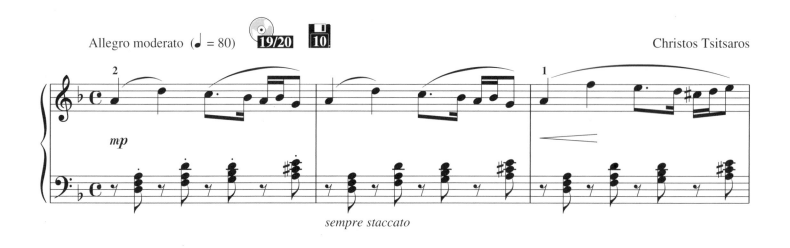

sempre staccato

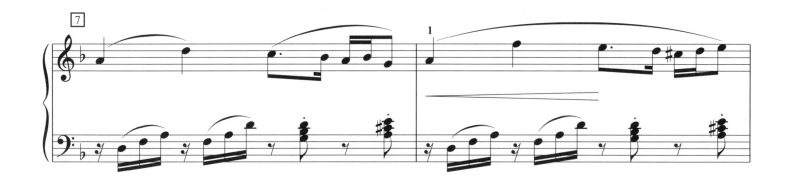

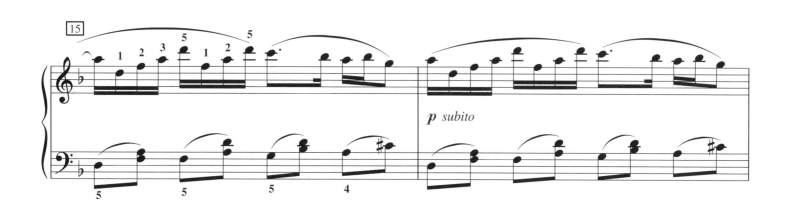

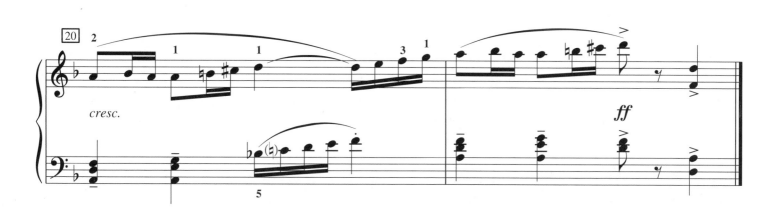

Cool Stepper

Carol Klose

23

For All The Blessings

Flowing (♩ = 96)

Barbara Gallagher

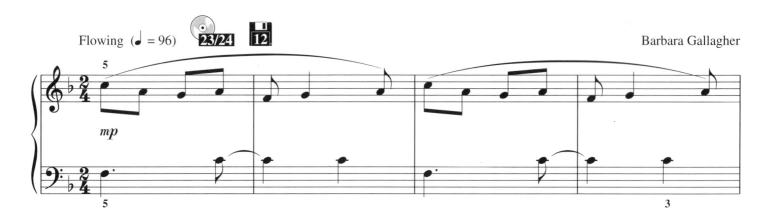

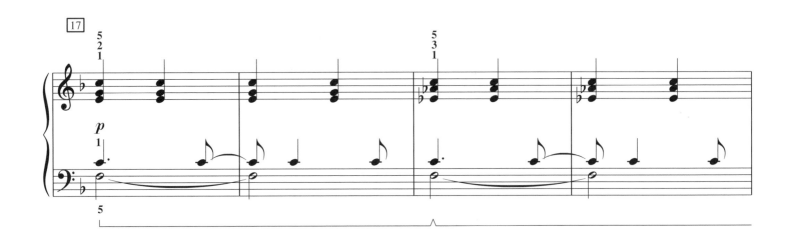

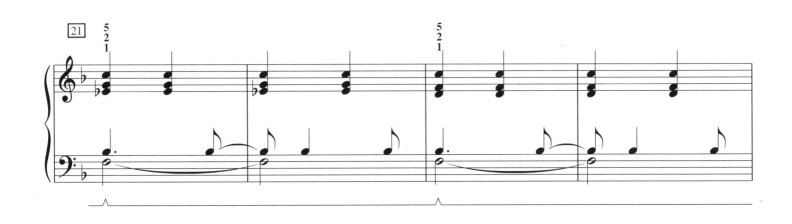

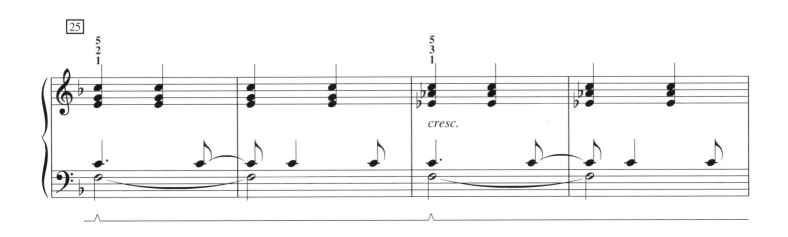

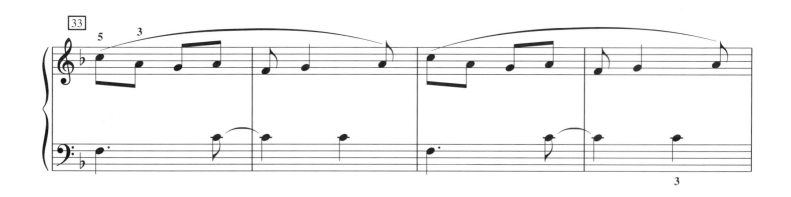

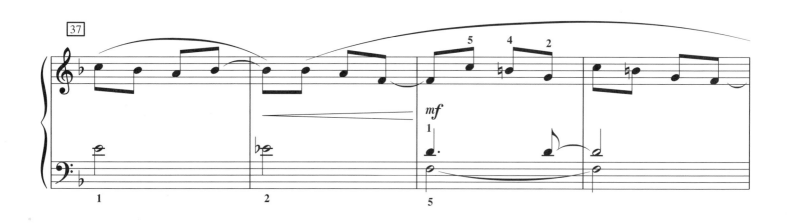

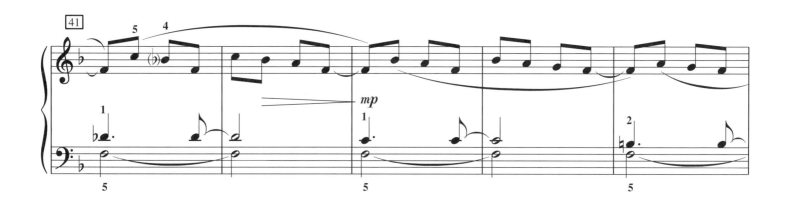

The Calm Before The Storm

Moderately flowing (♩ = 115)

Phillip Keveren

Use with Lesson Book 5, pg. 31

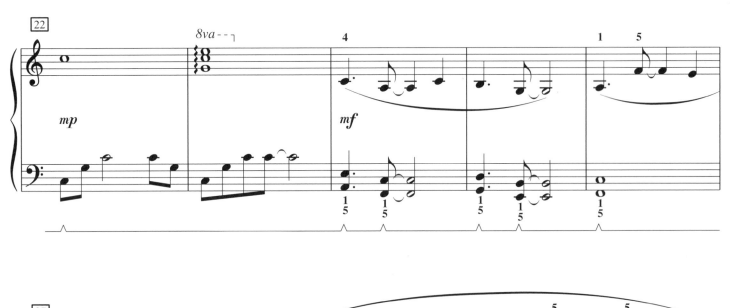

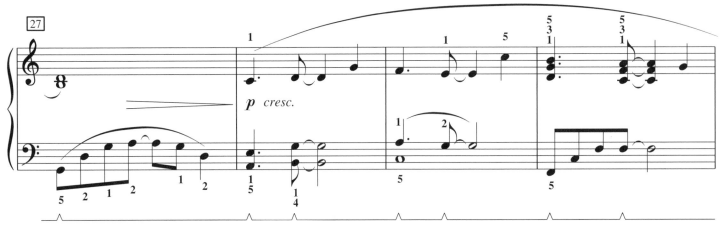

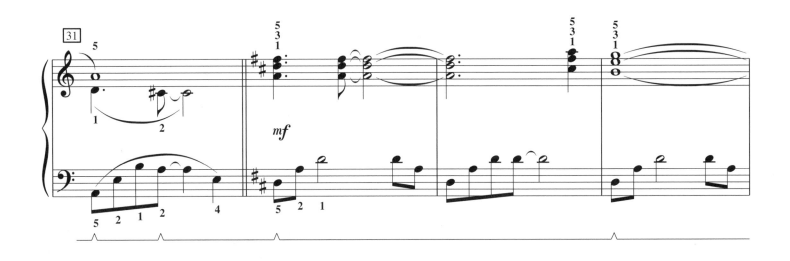

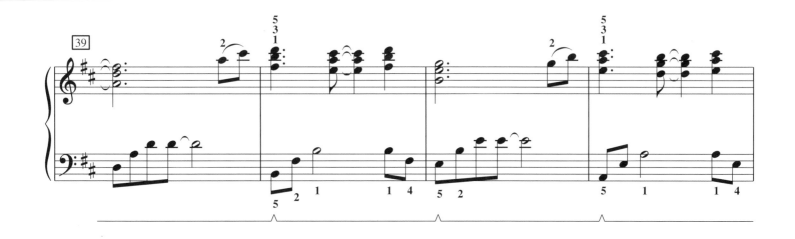

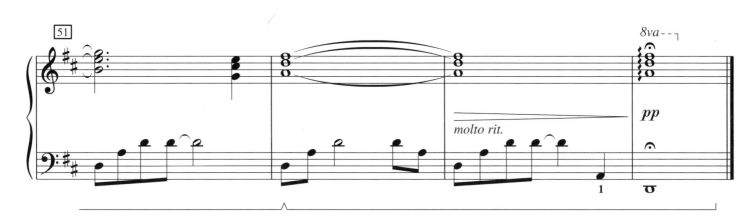

Toccatina

Vivace (♩ = 116)

Christos Tsitsaros

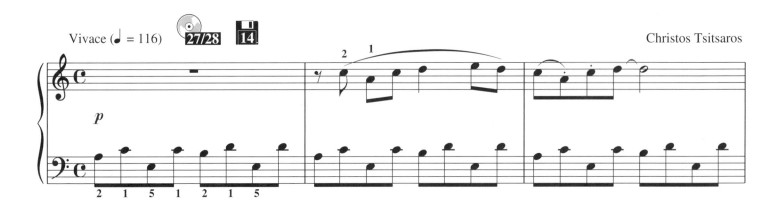

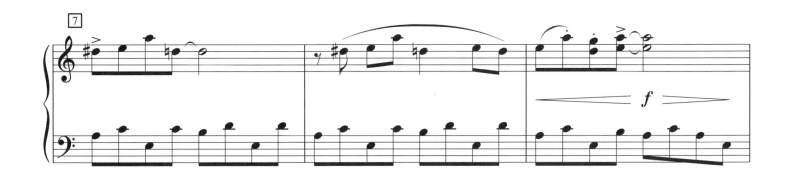

Prairie School Rag

Nocturne

Use with Lesson Book 5, pg. 40

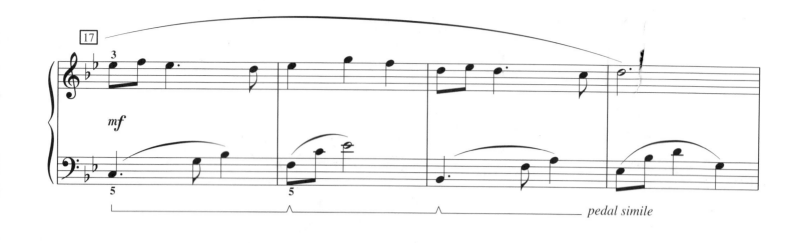

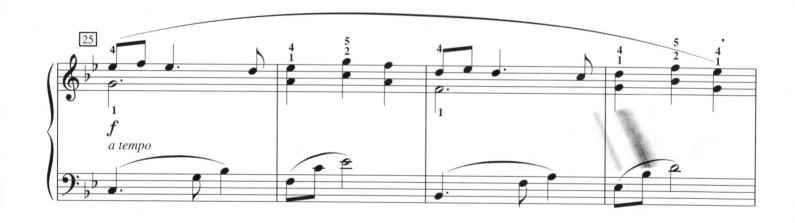

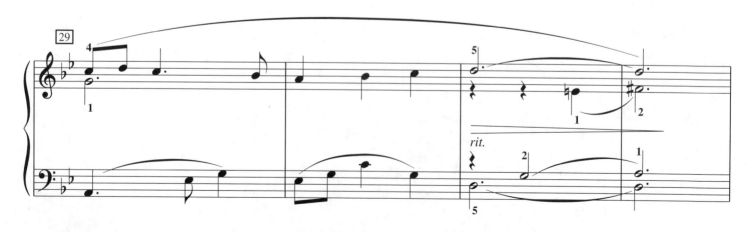

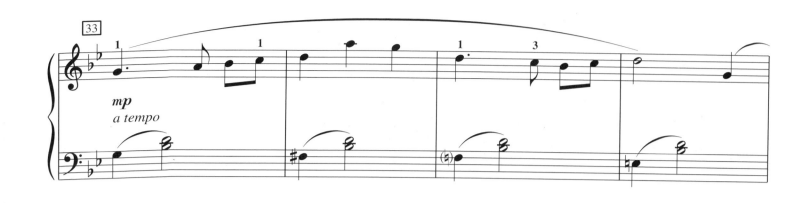

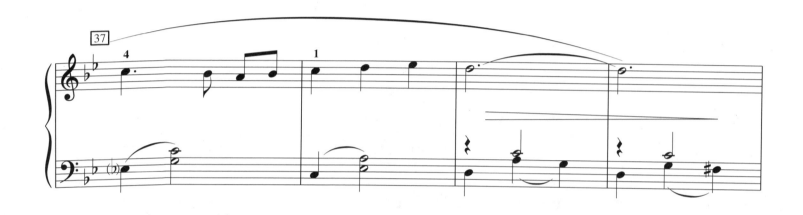

The Bass Man Walketh

Use with Lesson Book 5, pg. 42

38

D.S. al Coda

CODA

Remembrances

Tenderly ($\quad$ = 60)

Tony Caramia

41

Seagulls

Flowing (♩ = 114)

Christos Tsitsaros

Distant Waterfall

With motion ($\quad$ = 105)

Phillip Keveren

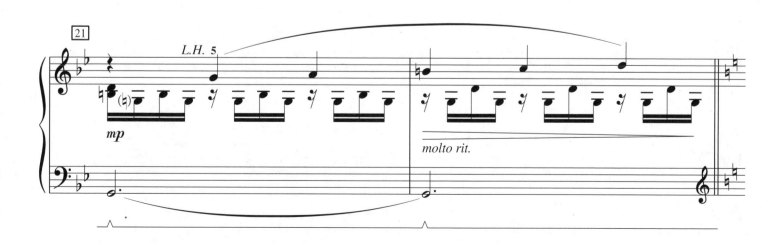

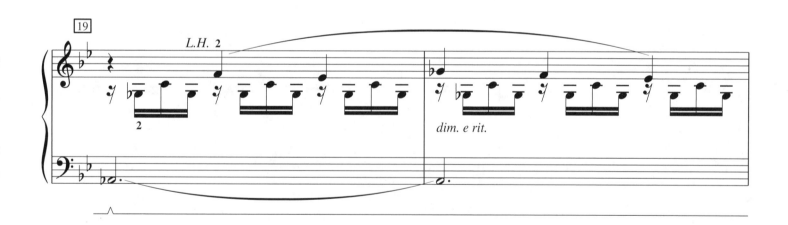

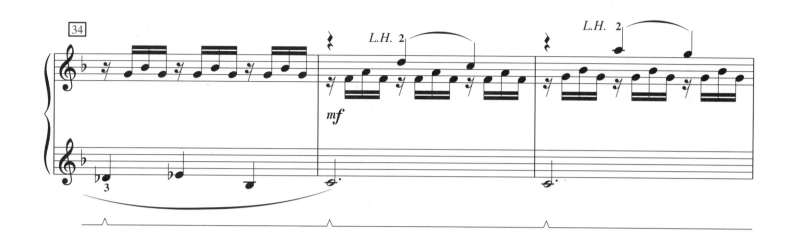

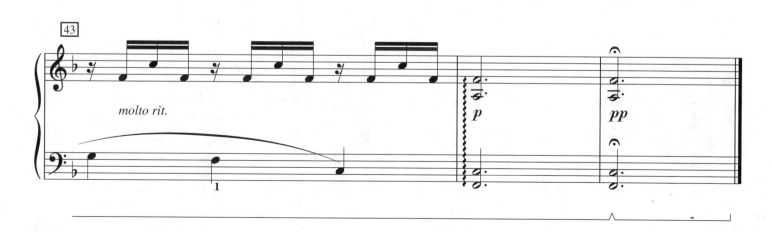

Method Authors

Barbara Kreader is Senior Editor for Educational Keyboard Products at Hal Leonard. A faculty member of Northwestern University's Division of Preparatory and Community Music from 1974-1985, Ms. Kreader has maintained her own independent piano studio from 1974 to the present. The editor of *Clavier* magazine from 1982-1988, Ms. Kreader acted as moderator for the three Baldwin/*Clavier* keyboard videoconferences, and has given workshops in over 85 cities in the United States and Canada. Ms. Kreader holds a M.M. in piano performance from Northwestern University where she studied piano with Laurence Davis and piano pedagogy with Frances Larimer.

A professor of music and a specialist in piano education at the University of North Texas, **Fred Kern** has been on the faculty of the College of Music since 1980. Dr. Kern is widely known as a clinician, author, composer, and arranger of texts and piano teaching materials. Most recently, he authored *The Adult Piano Method: Play by Choice* and the *More For Your Adult Method* series of supplementary music designed to coordinate with the most popular adult method in use today. Formerly on the faculty of Northwestern University, Dr. Kern holds graduate degrees in piano performance, music education, and piano pedagogy from Illinois Wesleyan, Northwestern University, and the University of Northern Colorado.

A multi-talented keyboard artist and composer, **Phillip Keveren** has composed original works in a variety of genres from piano solo to symphonic orchestra. His composition, "Presto Scherzo," was commissioned for the 1994 Conference on Piano Pedagogy. Formerly a composer, arranger, and senior staff member for the Yamaha Music Education System, Mr. Keveren gives frequent concerts and workshops for teachers and their students in the United States, Canada, Europe, and Asia. Mr. Keveren holds a B.M. in composition from California State University Northridge and a M.M. in composition from the University of Southern California.

Solos Series Composers

Bruce Berr, an independent piano teacher for over 20 years, is Coordinator of Piano Pedagogy at the Chicago Musical College at Roosevelt University. He has served on various committees for the National Conference on Piano Pedagogy, including the Director's Committee for the 1990 conference. Dr. Berr received his undergraduate and Master's degrees from Washington University in St. Louis and his Doctorate in piano performance and piano pedagogy from Northwestern University.

Bill Boyd has played piano professionally as both a solo performer and band member in hotels, supper clubs, and private clubs in New York and Long Island. Mr. Boyd is the composer of numerous jazz collections including the *Think Jazz* piano method and the *Jazz Starters* series for beginners. Mr. Boyd holds a Master's degree from Columbia University and taught junior high school band and stage band in Huntington, Long Island for over 20 years. Now retired from teaching, Mr. Boyd devotes all his time to arranging and composing.

Tony Caramia is associate professor of piano at Eastman School of Music, where, in addition to teaching piano primaries, he is the Director of Piano Pedagogy Studies and the coordinator of the Class Piano Program. Mr. Caramia is an active performer in both classical and jazz idioms, and has given workshops throughout the United States, Australia, and Europe.

Barbara Gallagher lives in Wilmington, NC, where she composes works for symphony orchestra, chamber ensembles, voice, piano, ballet, film and theatre. She holds a Bachelor of Music degree from N.C. School of the Arts, and was teaching fellow at The Juilliard School, where she earned her Master of Music degree. She has taught at Brunswick Community College and has judged for National Federation of Music Clubs and National Guild of Piano Teachers events. Currently, she teaches piano privately and is Director of Music for Immaculate Conception Catholic Church.

An accomplished pianist, teacher, and composer, **Carol Klose** holds piano performance degrees from Rosary College and Villa Schifanoia Graduate School of Fine Arts, Italy. Formerly on the faculty of the Wisconsin College/Conservatory of Music, Milwaukee, she teaches piano privately and is a frequent adjudicator and clinician. Additional published works include original compositions in the new NGPT Allison Contemporary Piano Collection, as well as numerous solos, duets, and folios arranged for students.

Jennifer Linn, an accomplished performer and composer in St. Louis, Missouri, has maintained a private studio for over 15 years. Her compositions have been selected for the National Federation of Music Clubs' list and twice featured in *Keys* magazine. Ms. Linn holds a M.M. from University of Missouri-Kansas City and is currently pursuing a DMA degree there.

Mona Rejino maintains a studio of 40 students in Carrollton, Texas, where she has taught students of all ages and levels for over 12 years. A member and former president of the Carrollton Music Teachers Association, Ms. Rejino received the CMTA "Teacher of the Year" award for outstanding membership. An active adjudicator and performer in the Dallas area, Ms. Rejino has recorded music for the *Adult Student* and *Pupil Savers*, which is produced and distributed by the National Piano Foundation. Ms. Rejino received her B.M. from West Texas State University and her M.M. in piano performance from the University of North Texas with Joseph Banowetz.

Christos Tsitsaros is currently Assistant Professor of Piano Pedagogy at the University of Illinois at Urbana-Champaign. The recipient of numerous scholarships and awards, Dr. Tsitsaros has appeared in recitals, chamber music concerts and as soloist in Europe and the United States. Dr. Tsitsaros holds the Diplôme Supérieur d'Execution from the École Normale de Musique de Paris, an Artist Diploma and M.M. degree from Indiana University, and a D.M.A. (piano performance) from the University of Illinois. A recent CD recording of his piano compositions is available through Centaur Records, Inc.